SECOND GRADE

The Superkids Take Off

BY

PLEASANT T. ROWLAND

STORIES WRITTEN BY

VALERIE TRIPP

ILLUSTRATED BY

NORM BENDELL

DEVELOPED BY

ROWLAND READING FOUNDATION

ZB **Zaner-Bloser**

A Highlights Company

ISBN 978-1-61436-580-8

Superkids is the exclusive registered trademark of Zaner-Bloser, Inc.

888.378.9258
zaner-bloser.com

Printed in the United States of America

9 2023

The SUPERKIDS Take Off

Cass

Oswald

Golly

Alf

Doc

Sal

Lily

Ms. Blossom

Icky

Tic

Tac

Toc

Frits

Ettabetta

Hot Rod

Contents

Unit 9

Unit 10

Unit 11

Chapter 21

Chapter 22

Unit 12

Chapter 23

Chapter 24

Unit 13

Unit 14

Unit 15

Chapter 29

Chapter 30

Unit 16

Chapter 31

Chapter 32

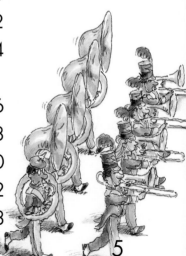

Chapter 17

The Worst News Ever

The Superkids were huddled around Toc's desk one morning before class began. They were upset.

"Time to begin, boys and girls!" said Ms. Blossom cheerfully. "Please be seated."

The Superkids slunk to their desks and flopped down.

"Dear me!" said Ms. Blossom. "What's the matter?"

"We've had the worst news <u>ever</u>," said Cass. "Our friends Gus and Gert have sold their gas station. They're going to retire."

"I see," said Ms. Blossom. "It is hard when friends move away."

"Gus and Gert are not leaving town," said Oswald. "They're just moving to an apartment near the park."

"Then what's the problem?" asked Ms. Blossom.

"This," said Toc.

Please adopt our dog Golly.

We are moving, and our new apartment house does not allow dogs.

E-mail:
gusngert@email.com

"If Golly is adopted by strangers, we may never see him again."

NoOOOOOo!!

7

Golly, What a Problem!

"Let's not waste time moping," said Ms. Blossom briskly. "We need a plan." She wrote on the flip chart:

What to do   Who will do it

"Now," she said, "what shall we do?"

"Hot Rod and I can ask Gus and Gert when they're moving," said Tic. "Then we'll know how much time we have to find a home for Golly."

"We can all ask our parents if we can adopt Golly," said Icky.

"We should write them letters," said Doc. "That's more grown-up."

"Let's write friends and neighbors too," added Frits.

"Lily and I could introduce Golly to the people at the apartment house," said Alf. "He's such a nice dog. Maybe they'll change their rules and let him move in."

Ms. Blossom wrote the Superkids' ideas on the chart. "Splendid," she said. "Let's get to work!"

请 妈妈 妈妈 请
请 爸爸 爸爸 请

Dear Baba and Mama,

Please, please, please, please,
please, can we adopt Golly?

Love,
Lily

P.S. Please?
P.P.S. XOXOXO

请 请 妈妈
请 请 爸爸

Dear Ms. Gibson,
Our class knows a
very nice dog called
Golly. He needs a
place to live. Could
Golly come and live on
your farm?
Please write back
and let us know.
Love,
Tɔc

10

I am lonely.
Let's adopt Golly.
Printed for
Coconut by Cass.

Dear Grandpop,
Golly is a nice
dog. Can he come
Live with you at
your cabin?
Love,
Frits

Golly

Mom and Dad!
HELP! Gus and Gert are moving, and they can't take Golly with them. We've GOT to adopt him or someone else might, and they might take Golly far away, and then we'd NEVER see him again. That would be TERRIBLE!!!!!

Please say that we can adopt Golly. I will never ask for anything ever again in my WHOLE LIFE if you say yes. Say YES!
                    Love, Love, Love
              Ettabetta X X X X X X X

Dear Mama and Papa,

Golly needs a new home. May I adopt him? I promise that I will feed him, walk him, give him baths, and brush his teeth.

I will take good care of Golly, just like you take good care of me, and I will love Golly, just like I love you.

From,

Sal

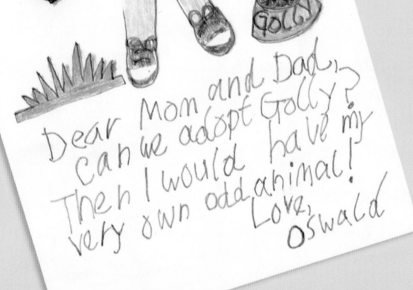

Dear Mom and Dad, can we adopt Golly? Then I would have my very own odd animal!
Love,
Oswald

Great Dog Golly

After school, Hot Rod and Tic ran to Gus and Gert's gas station. Lily and Alf came too.

"Gert!" gasped Tic. "When are you moving?"

"Next week," said Gert.

"That doesn't give us much time," said Hot Rod.

"We're trying to find a home nearby for Golly," said Tic.

"So that we can still see him," added Hot Rod.

"Gus and I feel terrible about parting with Golly," said Gert. "You kids are great to help."

"Well, Golly is a <u>great</u> dog," said Alf. "May Lily and I take him to your new apartment house? We think that if people met Golly, they might change their rules and let him live there with you."

"It's worth a try," said Gus.

"Come on, Golly," said Lily. "Let's go show them just how great a dog you are."

No Good News

Day after day, the Superkids hurried to school hoping that someone would have good news about Golly. But no one did. Everyone loved Golly, but no one could adopt him.

"My parents said no because we already have a cat," said Cass.

"My brother Ben is allergic to dogs," said Oswald.

"So is my mother," said Tic.

"My parents travel too much," said Sal.

My parents said no because we already have a cat.

"The people at the apartment house said Golly was nice, but they couldn't change the rules for him," said Alf.

"Grandpop said Golly could live at his cabin," said Frits, "but only during the summer when Golly could stay outside."

"You tried hard, boys and girls," said Ms. Blossom. "But I am afraid you're going to have to say goodbye to Golly. Gus called me today. A friend of his who lives far away has said that he will adopt Golly. So Golly will be leaving a week from Saturday."

The Superkids were crushed. They sat at their desks, all thinking the same thing—how could they <u>ever</u> say goodbye to Golly?

MS. BLOSSO

17

Chapter 18

Good News + Bad News = Medium News

Toc burst into the classroom waving a letter above her head. "I have some good news and some bad news," she said. "Which do you want to hear first?"

"Tell us the good news!" said the Superkids.

"OK!" said Toc. "This letter is from Ms. Gibson. She wrote that she'd love to have Golly come live on her farm."

"Hooray!" shouted the Superkids happily.

"That _is_ good news!" said Sal.

"The bad news is that Ms. Gibson's farm is one hour away from here," said Toc. "We won't be able to see Golly very often."

"Oh," groaned the Superkids unhappily.

"That's _bad_ news!" said Frits.

"Well, it's not terrible," said Doc. "Golly will be far away, but he'll be living with someone nice. He'll be happy."

"Yes," said Toc, "and I'm sure Ms. Gibson would be glad if we visited Golly sometimes. At least we won't have to say goodbye to him forever."

"I guess the good news and the bad news add up to medium news," said Alf,

Golly's New Home

Saturday morning, the Superkids met at the gas station to help Gus and Gert deliver Golly to the farm. Gus and Gert invited Ms. Blossom to come along too.

Ms. Blossom had never met Golly before. She knelt down and stroked Golly's long ears. "You're a handsome dog," she said to Golly. "I can see why the kids love you."

Golly wagged his tail and smiled his goofy, doggy smile at Ms. Blossom.

Everyone was quiet on the ride to the farm. Golly seemed to understand that something serious was happening. He stretched out on the floor of the van and put his nose on his paws. His eyes and ears were alert. When they arrived at the farm, Golly followed Gert out of the van.

"Well, hello there, you fine fellow!" said Ms. Gibson as she hugged Golly. "Welcome to the farm."

Golly wagged his tail and leaned against Ms. Gibson in such a friendly way that the Superkids had to smile.

On the Farm

The first farm animal Golly met was Ms. Gibson's horse, Brown Sugar. The Superkids saw that Golly and Brown Sugar seemed to like each other right away.

Then Golly and the Superkids went to the pond. It was frozen, so the Superkids went skating on it in their boots. Golly spun around in circles, which he seemed to enjoy a lot.

Next, Sal and Golly went to see the pig. Golly made friends with the pig.

When Golly went into the barn, a loud parade of chickens followed him.

Ms. Gibson introduced Golly to Baby. Golly did <u>not</u> make friends with Baby.

Ms. Gibson let the Superkids use her toboggan. Ms. Blossom was a little nervous about going so fast, but Golly loved it!

After the toboggan ride, Golly made a wonderful discovery. He had his very own door so he could go in and out of the house whenever he wanted to.

Then the kids had a snowball fight. Golly kept catching snowballs in his mouth!

The Superkids were happy because they could tell that Ms. Gibson would always be very kind to Golly.

Gifts for Golly

"We'll have to leave pretty soon, kids," said Gert. "You had better give Golly your gifts now."

"Good old Golly," said Frits. "Here's a new water bowl for you with your name on it. We hope that whenever you use it, you'll think of us."

"We got you a new bed too," said Doc. "Maybe you'll dream about us when you sleep on it."

"We bought you some new balls to chase," said Sal. "And these are real balls, not snowballs!"

"We'll come visit you in the spring," said Tic, "and play catch."

"I drew a picture of all of us," said Oswald. "Ms. Gibson can tack it on the wall by your food bowl. That way, you won't forget us."

One by one, the Superkids hugged Golly goodbye. Then they all climbed sadly into the van. As the van pulled away, the Superkids waved.

"Goodbye, Golly!" they called. "We love you!"

A Letter from Golly

Dear Superkids,

Ruff, ruff, ruff and hello! Ms. Gibson and I are getting along fine on the farm. I've been here a week now, and every day has taught me something new.

I've learned the hard way that cows can move pretty fast when they want to, so it's better to stay out of their way.

Sheep and lambs stay out of <u>my</u> way. I try to be friendly, but they seem to think I'm herding them when I've just stopped by for a nice visit.

Ms. Gibson and I work hard. Well, Ms. Gibson works hard, and I keep her company. We milk the cows, toss hay to the horses, and scatter corn for the chickens.

One of my most important jobs is eating leftovers. Ms. Gibson says I do that job <u>very</u> well.

It is pretty quiet here on the farm in the winter. I hope you'll visit again in the spring. I miss you. Ms. Gibson and I send our love.

Your old friend,
Golly

Chapter 19

Homework

Tac walked carefully in her clunky boots. She held a piece of paper in front of her with both hands.

"What's that?" asked Oswald.

"My homework," said Tac. "I'm holding it so it won't get crumpled in my backpack."

"Homework?" asked Oswald.

"Oh, Oswald," said Tac. "Did you forget? Ms. Blossom asked us to draw our favorite thing from our Book Club book and write a sentence about it."

"I _did_ forget," Oswald moaned. "What'll I do?"

"Sit down on the bench and draw something right now," said Tac. "What was your favorite thing in the story?"

Oswald shrugged. "I don't know," he said. "I didn't finish it."

"Well, then," said Tac, "you'd better just draw a horse, like I did."

Oswald yanked a piece of paper and a pencil out of his backpack and quickly sketched a running horse. Under it, he scribbled:

horses are fast

"That's good," said Tac, without even looking at Oswald's drawing. "Here comes the bus. Let's go."

31

Poor Oswald?

One of the things the Superkids loved most about second grade was Book Club. In Book Club, they got to read real chapter books with Ms. Blossom. Sometimes they did a project in class about the book they were reading. Sometimes they did homework.

Today, Ms. Blossom said, "Who would like to share their Book Club homework?"

Tac raised her hand. She saw Oswald trying to smooth his paper, which was wet and wrinkled. Smoothing it was a mistake, because he smeared his drawing.

Ms. Blossom picked up Oswald's paper. "May I share your work?" she asked.

Oswald nodded unhappily.

Poor Oswald, thought Tac. Ms. Blossom was always kind, but Tac was sure she'd say that Oswald's work was messy.

"Class," said Ms. Blossom. "Look at Oswald's horse. It is blurry and tilted, so we can tell that it is running downhill fast. Oswald's handwriting is slanted, so that the way the words <u>look</u> shows what they <u>mean</u>." Ms. Blossom smiled at Oswald. "Your work gives us a feeling of speed and excitement. It's splendid."

"Thanks!" said Oswald. He grinned at Tac as if to say, "Phew!"

A Fat, Four-Legged Frog

It's not fair! thought Tac. *I did my homework properly. I didn't dash it off at the last minute, like Oswald!* But now that Tac had really looked at Oswald's drawing, she had to admit that it was better than hers. Compared with Oswald's horse, her horse looked like a fat, four-legged frog stuck in the muck. Even her sentence, "I like horses," was as dull as mud.

Tac slumped in her seat so that Ms. Blossom would not call on her.

"Anyone who'd like extra time to read is welcome to join the Lunch Bunch today," said Ms. Blossom. "We'll meet here in the classroom." Ms. Blossom held up her pointer finger and made a circle in the air. The circle got wider and wider as she raised up her arm. "Remember, we become better readers by reading a book again and again until our reading is just . . . "

"SPLENDID!" shouted all the students.

Tac sat up straight and smiled. Ms. Blossom had given her a great idea!

The Lunch Bunch

Tac opened the classroom door slowly. She had never come to a meeting of the Lunch Bunch before, so she wasn't quite sure how it worked. She was glad when Ms. Blossom said, "Well, hello, Tac. Welcome to the Lunch Bunch. What would you like to work on today?"

"Is it OK if I do homework?" asked Tac.

"Sure," said Ms. Blossom. "If you need any help, just ask me."

"Tac?" Oswald said. "I thought you'd finished your homework."

"I did," said Tac. "But I want to do it over again to make it better. It may take me a while. I'm not good at drawing, like you are."

"Well, I'm not good at reading, like you are," said Oswald. "I'm here because I need extra time to read the book."

Tac grinned. She made a circle in the air with her finger, just as Ms. Blossom had. "If you <u>read</u> again and again," she said, "and I <u>draw</u> again and again, soon our work will be just . . ."

SPLENDID!

Better Than Splendid

The rest of the class came in from recess with red cheeks and smelling of the cold, fresh air. Tac looked up. She was surprised that recess was over already. She had been so busy working on her homework that she had not noticed the time going by.

"You should have come outside," Ettabetta said to Tac. "We made a snow fort. It was really fun."

But Tac was happy with the choice she'd made to stay inside with the Lunch Bunch. The floor around her desk was covered with crumpled papers, but at last she was pleased with her work.

Tac was even more pleased when Ms. Blossom said, "Boys and girls, isn't it wonderful how we are all different? Some of us work quickly. Some of us work slowly. I am proud of Tac because she tried again and again to make her homework better."

Ms. Blossom put a little flowerpot on Tac's desk. "Tac's work is so good," said Ms. Blossom, "that I'll use a special word to describe it." She clipped a note to the flower that said: specTACular

Chapter 20

Ms. Blossom's Surprise

One morning, Ms. Blossom said, "Boys and girls, I have a surprise for you. This Friday, we are going on a field trip to the Natural History Museum."

"Hooray!" cheered all the Superkids.

"Will we see woolly mammoths and great blue whales and polar bears?" asked Alf.

"Yes," said Ms. Blossom. "We'll not only see them, we'll sleep with them! We're going to spend the night at the museum."

"WOW!" shouted the Superkids. They clapped and whistled.

"Here are your permission slips. Be sure to get them signed and bring them in before Friday," said Ms. Blossom. "We'll leave for the museum right after school, so remember to bring a sleeping bag, your pajamas, and your toothbrush with you that morning."

Oswald poked Sal. "I'm going to pack my dinosaur pajamas," he said.

"I'm going to pack my—" Sal stopped. He changed what he was going to say. Instead, he said, "Flashlight."

Hair Combs

"What's that big lump in your backpack?" Icky asked Sal as they were riding the bus to the museum on Friday afternoon.

"It's my, um, my pajamas," said Sal. He quickly pointed to Lily. "Look who brought a pillow! What a baby!"

"I know," agreed Icky. "And the pillowcase has brides on it. Yuck!"

"Hey, Lily," called Sal. "Knock, knock."

"Who's there?" said Lily.

"Hair combs," said Sal.

"Hair combs who?" said Lily.

"Hair combs the bride!" said Sal.

"Yes," teased Icky. "And she's all over your pillowcase!"

Icky and Sal laughed and laughed.

Lily was annoyed.

"Don't pay any attention to them," Cass said to her. "You were smart to bring a pillow."

Lily smiled at Cass. "Let's put our sleeping bags next to each other tonight," she said. "You can share my pillow if you want."

"Thanks!" said Cass.

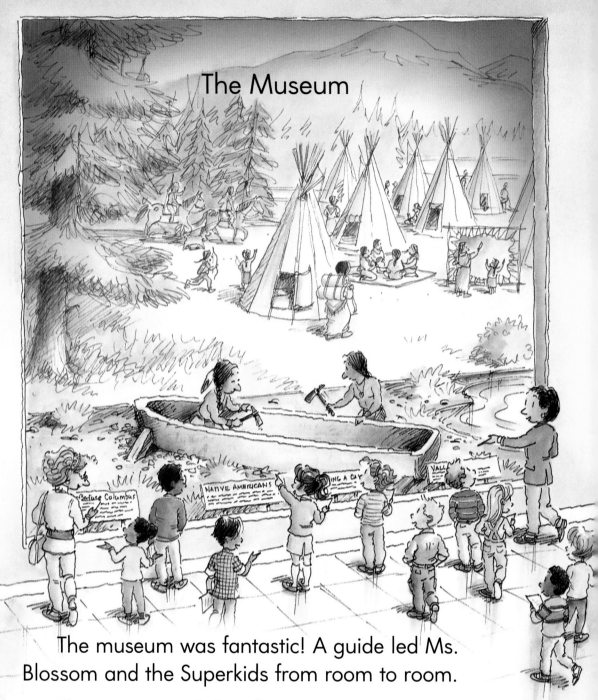

The Museum

The museum was fantastic! A guide led Ms. Blossom and the Superkids from room to room.

They saw an exhibit about Native Americans carving canoes.

They tasted buffalo meat and smelled the sweet
scent of flowers that grow in the rain forest.

They heard recordings of whale
songs and elephant calls.

Icky touched a
tiger's tooth.

Lily and Tac touched fossils.

But <u>no</u> <u>one</u> touched
the tarantula!

After dinner, the girls brushed their teeth in the restroom. Lily asked Cass, "What did you like best?"

"Oh, the giant white polar bear!" said Cass. "Wasn't it <u>huge</u>?"

"Mmm-hmm," said Lily. She didn't want to admit that the polar bear gave her the creeps. She shivered now as she remembered the moment she first saw it. The polar bear had sharp claws, yellow teeth, and a hungry expression in its icy eyes. It wasn't even in a glass case but standing up on its legs right in the room. Lily had been glad to get away from it.

Lily Gets Lost

The Superkids spread out their sleeping bags in a room with a big blue whale hanging from the ceiling. Lily was happy. The whale looked kind and protective. She felt safe cuddled up beneath it with Cass's head on the pillow beside her. Soon she fell asleep.

A while later, Lily woke up. "Cass," she said softly. She jiggled Cass's arm. "I need to go to the restroom. Please come with me." But Cass just mumbled and rolled over, so Lily got up and tiptoed to the restroom by herself.

Getting <u>to</u> the restroom didn't take long. But on the way back, Lily's feet began to get cold. *I've been walking for a long time,* Lily thought. *I hope I haven't taken a wrong turn.* Suddenly . . .

47

48

"EEK!" Lily shrieked.

<u>She</u> <u>was</u> <u>in</u> <u>the</u> <u>polar-bear</u> <u>room!</u>

Lily couldn't breathe. The terrible white bear seemed to be leaning toward her, reaching out with its sharp, cruel claws to grab her.

"Lily!" someone whispered.

"EEK!" Lily shrieked again, just about jumping out of her skin.

"It's me," said Sal. "I'm sorry! I didn't mean to scare you. I heard you yell, so I came to see what was wrong."

"I'm <u>lost</u>," cried Lily. "Get me OUT of here!"

"Follow me!" said Sal, and they began to run.

Bailey Bear

Sal led Lily back to the whale room. They stood in the doorway for a minute.

"Please stop crying," said Sal.

"I c-c-c-can't," sobbed Lily. "I don't like sleeping away from home, and I <u>hate</u> that horrible polar bear."

"I don't like sleepovers either," said Sal. "Here. Take this." He thrust a fat, stuffed bear into Lily's hands.

"What's this?" gulped Lily between her tears.

"It's my bear, Bailey," said Sal. "I hid him in my sleeping bag because I didn't want anyone to tease me about him. But he helps me feel safe. You can keep him tonight. He'll make <u>you</u> feel safe."

Lily looked at Bailey. "Sal," she said, with a little smile. "Bailey is a <u>polar</u> bear."

"Well, yes," said Sal. "But see how nice and soft he is? You can't be scared of Bailey!"

"No, I can't," said Lily. She hugged Bailey, then handed him back to Sal.

"Thanks," she said. "But I'm OK now." Lily grinned. "Besides, I've got all those brides on my pillowcase to keep me company, right?"

Sal grinned back and said, "Right!"

Chapter 21

The 100 Party

Ms. Blossom said, "Next Friday, our town will be one hundred years old. How shall we celebrate?"

"Let's have a 100 Party," said Hot Rod. "It can be one hundred minutes long."

"We can dress up like kids from one hundred years ago," said Tic.

"Yes!" said Cass. "The girls can wear long dresses and big hair bows, and the boys can wear suits and ties."

"No way!" shouted the boys.

"Suits are uncomfortable," said Icky.

"Besides," added Alf. "We don't want to dress up like one-hundred-year-old guys!"

"Right!" said Sal. "Why can't we dress up as people who are cool and famous now?"

"Because that has nothing to do with being one hundred years old," said Ettabetta.

"I have an idea," said Frits. "We can dress up as people we admire. They can be real or make-believe. But they should be so cool that they'll still be famous one hundred years from now."

"Splendid," said Ms. Blossom, and all the Superkids agreed.

100 ~~Ice-Cream~~ *pine* Cones

"What will we do at the One Hundred Party?" asked Lily.

"We'll eat one hundred ice-cream cones!" said Hot Rod.

"Hooray!" everyone cheered.

Ms. Blossom laughed. "I'm afraid one hundred ice-cream cones would cost too much money," she said. "But perhaps you could bring in one hundred <u>free</u> things. We'll use them to decorate the room."

The children liked that idea. They chatted with one another and decided to bring things like leaves, pebbles, sticks, apple seeds, feathers, and acorns.

Ettabetta said to Hot Rod, "We can bring pine cones."

"OK," said Hot Rod. "We can't eat pine cones, but at least they won't melt!"

55

Super Suits

After lunch, Alf spoke to Alec in the media center.

"For the party, I want to be Neil Armstrong," said Alf. "I admire him because he was the first person to walk on the moon. I'm sure he'll be famous one hundred years from now. Will you help me figure out how to make a cool astronaut suit?"

"Sure!" said Alec.

Alf and Alec looked at pictures of astronauts on the Internet. Then Alec drew a space-suit costume for Alf and labeled the parts.

"This suit is super!" said Alf. "Hey! Would you like to be an astronaut too? You could be Buzz Aldrin. He walked on the moon with Neil Armstrong. Aldrin and Armstrong, Alec and Alf!"

"That's cool," said Alec. "All our names begin with A. And that's A-OK, as the astronauts say."

Cinderella

"Who are you going to be?" Ettabetta asked Doc.

"It's a secret," said Doc as she tied her scarf over her head and under her chin.

"You can tell <u>me</u>," said Ettabetta as she tied <u>her</u> scarf over her head and under her chin, just like Doc.

"I'm going to be Cinderella," said Doc.

"Oh," said Ettabetta. "How come you admire Cinderella?"

"Well," said Doc, "even though her stepsisters are mean to her, she isn't mean to them. She even forgives them in the end."

"They <u>are</u> mean," said Ettabetta. "I've always wondered why Cinderella asked her fairy godmother to help her go to the <u>ball</u>. If I were Cinderella, I'd ask my fairy godmother to teach me how to use her magic wand. Then I'd turn those sisters into snakes."

"But then you wouldn't get to marry the prince and live happily ever after," Doc said.

"Well," said Ettabetta. "I'd rather be a fairy godmother's helper than marry a silly prince!"

100 Is <u>A</u> <u>LOT</u>!

61

Chapter 22

Not So Special

Ettabetta and Hot Rod brought the pine cones that they'd collected to school in a big basket. Oswald and Doc strung their one hundred leaves on a long piece of string. They hung the streamer of leaves across the windows of the classroom.

"Ooh," said all the students. The leaves were a bit crumbly, but they looked pretty.

"What a good idea!" said Ettabetta.

"Thanks," said Doc with a smile.

But Doc did <u>not</u> smile when she came back after lunch. She saw that Ettabetta had made a streamer of pine cones and hung it across the windows too, right above the leaves.

"Don't the pine cones look great?" Ettabetta asked Doc.

"Mmm-hmm," said Doc coolly. She and Oswald had been proud of their idea. But their streamer of leaves didn't seem so special anymore with the pine cones hanging over it. Doc tried not to care that Ettabetta had copied her idea, but it sort of bugged her.

Spacemen

The day of the party was unusually warm. As Alf and Alec walked to school, the sun glinted off the foil on their space suits and made them look dazzling.

"Let's pretend we're walking on the moon!" shouted Alf. Both boys went leaping down the street.

But they soon slowed down. Their snow pants and jackets made them sweaty and itchy, and the foil on their space suits made them extra hot.

"Yikes," panted Alf as they got to school. "Our space suits <u>look</u> cool, but they sure don't <u>feel</u> cool. I don't want to roast all day."

"I've got an idea," said Alec. "Come on."

A few minutes later, Alf and Alec came out of the boys' room looking thinner—and a lot more comfortable.

"Our space suits still look great," said Alec. "And they're even <u>cooler</u> than before!"

Copycat

Doc walked to school slowly and carefully. She was dressed as Cinderella, and she didn't want her tiara to fall off. She was also a bit teetery on her feet because she was wearing her mother's sparkly bedroom slippers. They were the closest thing to glass slippers she could find, and they were too big.

"Wait up, Doc!" she heard someone call.

Doc stopped, turned, and gasped. Ettabetta was running toward her with a wand in her hand, <u>and she was dressed in a ball gown too</u>!

"Surprise!" said Ettabetta. "I'm your fairy godmother!"

"What?" snapped Doc.

"Your fairy godmother!" Ettabetta said, waving her wand. "You know, I'm the one with all the magic powers who helps you go to the ball!"

"But you <u>can't</u> be," said Doc.

"What do you mean?" asked Ettabetta. "Why not?"

"Because Cinderella was <u>my</u> idea," said Doc. "And I'm tired of you copycatting me and stealing my ideas all the time!"

67

Someone You Admire

Ettabetta was surprised. "I thought you'd like it that I was your fairy godmother," she said.

Doc took a deep breath. "I'm sorry I yelled at you," she said. "But I felt angry when I saw your costume. I felt like you stole my idea."

"Cinderella doesn't belong to you," said Ettabetta. "I admire the fairy godmother, so I can choose to be her."

"Yes," said Doc. "I just really wish you admired someone else."

"I admire <u>you</u>," said Ettabetta. "That's why I copy you."

"Oh!" said Doc. She was quiet for a moment. Then she said, "It's nice that you admire me, but I still wish you wouldn't copy me."

"I'm sorry," said Ettabetta. "I should have asked you first about being the fairy godmother. Can you forgive me the way Cinderella forgave her sisters?"

"I think so," Doc said with a little smile. "Come on. Let's go, or we'll be late for the ball."

The Best Party Ever

Everyone agreed that the 100 Party was the best party ever. Ms. Blossom borrowed jump ropes from the gym teacher. It was quite a sight to see two astronauts jumping rope right next to Abraham Lincoln, George Washington, and Cinderella and her fairy godmother. "Ninety-six, ninety-seven, ninety-eight, ninety-nine, ONE HUNDRED!" they panted. "We did it! We did it! We jumped one hundred jumps!"

Ms. Blossom brought orange-juice pops for everyone to eat while they were cooling off.

But the best part of all was Frits and Toc's surprise.

"We couldn't find feathers," said Frits, "so we brought something else instead. Are you ready?"

"Yes!" shouted the Superkids.

Toc and Frits held the ends of a folded sheet. "One, two, three!" they counted. They tossed the sheet high into the air, and out flew one hundred origami birds!

"Ooh!" said the Superkids.

71

Chapter 23

Basketball Season Begins

One day after lunch, Alec said, "The snow has finally melted. Let's play soccer." He tapped a soccer ball to Sal with his knee.

"I don't think we can," said Sal. "The soccer field is underwater. Look at those puddles."

"The blacktop is dry," said Tic. "Let's play basketball."

"YES!" cheered all the Superkids, except Alec.

Tic grabbed a basketball, twirled around, and shot. Swish! It went through the basket.

"Good shot," said Sal. "Let's choose up sides. Tic and I will be captains."

"OK," said Tic. "Alec, you can be on my team."

"Uh, no thanks," said Alec. "I'm . . . I'm going inside with the Lunch Bunch."

"You are?" asked Lily. "A minute ago you wanted to play soccer."

"Well, I just remembered that I didn't finish my homework," said Alec.

"What homework?" asked Hot Rod. "We didn't have—"

But Alec had already run off.

73

A Note for Alec

Alec was sitting on his stool in art class when he felt someone poke him. It was Frits. Frits handed Alec a note, then continued to walk to the pencil sharpener without saying a word.

Alec unfolded the note. It said:

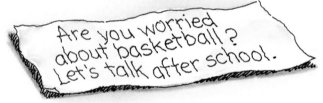

Alec frowned at Frits and shook his head no. Then Alec crumpled the note into a ball and tossed it into the trash can.

"Good shot, Alec!" said Tic. "My team needs a shooter like you. Can you play with us tomorrow?"

Alec's face turned red. "Maybe," he said. Then he looked at Frits with a panicked expression and whispered, "Maybe we <u>should</u> meet after school."

Frits grinned and said, "OK."

Shrimps

After school, Frits was waiting for Alec on the blacktop. He had a basketball tucked under his arm. "I think I know why you don't want to play basketball," Frits said. "It's because you're too short, right?"

"Well, right," said Alec.

"I know how you feel because I'm a shrimp too," said Frits. He bounced the ball to Alec. "It's a pain being short. We have to run twice as hard as the tall kids. We always have to stand in the front row. People think we're younger than we really are, just because we're shrimps."

Alec nodded and bounced the ball back to Frits.

"So, you could avoid basketball for the rest of your life," said Frits, "or you could—"

"Play basketball and be awful," said Alec. "I can never score. The basket is just too high for me."

"It's high for me too," said Frits. "But I know a secret shot that works for us shrimps. I'll teach you."

The Squat Shot

"Watch," said Frits. He bent his knees and held the basketball between his legs. Then—swoop! He lifted himself up onto his toes and tossed the ball underhand at the basket. In it went—sloop! Frits grinned at Alec. "Score!" he said.

Alec shook his head. "I can't shoot like <u>that</u>," he said. "It looks <u>weird</u>. Don't people laugh at you?"

Frits shrugged. "If they do, they stop laughing when I sink my shot," he said. He threw the ball to Alec. "Try it."

Alec went down into a squat holding the ball. "I feel like a frog," he said.

"Just shoot," said Frits.

Alec shot. The ball went so high that it sailed over the top of the backboard.

"That's OK," said Frits. "Don't be discouraged."

"Discouraged?" said Alec. "I've <u>never</u> come that close to making a basket! I want to try that shot again!"

The Shrimp Shot

   All week, Alec and Frits met to practice the weird-looking squat shot. Pretty soon Alec was making almost as many baskets as Frits.

   "Are you ready to play in the game today?" Frits asked Alec on Friday.

   "I guess so," said Alec, but he wasn't so sure.

   The two boys were on the same team. Alec was glad to see that no one laughed when Frits made his squat shot. But whenever Alec got the ball himself, he passed it straight to Frits.

   Finally, when the game was nearly over, Frits passed the ball back to Alec and said, "No, <u>you</u> take it."

   "Shoot!" yelled everyone on the team.

"Here goes," Alec said to himself. He squatted, held the ball in both hands, and then heaved it underhand toward the basket. Swish! The ball slipped through the basket smooth as could be.

"Nice!" said Frits as the team cheered.

"That squat shot is weird," said Alec, "but it works."

"Yep," said Frits. "It's a sure shot."

"No," said Alec. "It's a <u>shrimp</u> shot."

Chapter 24

Mr. Kumasi

The Superkids walked into their classroom chatting and laughing as usual. Then, suddenly, everybody was silent. A tall, smiling man stood in front of the room. Ms. Blossom was not there! The Superkids were flabbergasted.

"Good morning, ladies and gentlemen," the man said. "I am Mr. Kumasi."

"Good morning," the Superkids said shyly.

"Please take your seats," said Mr. Kumasi.

"Excuse me, Mr. Kumasi," said Icky politely as everyone sat. "But where is Ms. Blossom?"

"I am sorry to say that Ms. Blossom has the flu," said Mr. Kumasi. "I will be your substitute teacher until she returns."

The Superkids looked at each other with worried faces. They loved Ms. Blossom, and it made them sad to hear that she was not feeling well. Also, they were nervous. Mr. Kumasi seemed nice, but it felt wrong to have someone who was a stranger in charge of their class.

They all agreed with Icky when he said, "I hope Ms. Blossom feels better soon."

Thursday

Mr. Kumasi taped a map of Africa to the board so everybody could see.

The Superkids looked at one another. This was not the way Ms. Blossom began the day.

Icky said politely, "Ms. Blossom always begins with reading."

"Does she?" said Mr. Kumasi. "Well, today we'll do something different. Watch and listen."

Mr. Kumasi pointed to the map. "I'm from Ghana," he said. "In Ghana, children are often named for the day of the week on which they were born." He wrote the days of the week on the board in big letters. "Everyone, please come stand under your day."

"What if we don't know what day we were born on?" asked Sal.

"Then look at the calendar, and use the day your birthday is <u>this</u> year," said Mr. Kumasi.

The Superkids felt discombobulated. They tripped over one another as they went to the board.

"This is weird!" Tic whispered.

"Yes," giggled Tac. "But I like being Thursday."

85

Football

"It's a beautiful day," said Mr. Kumasi. "Let's go outside."

Icky started to say, "But Ms. Blossom never—"

"Shh!" hissed the rest of the kids. Ms. Blossom never gave the class recess that early in the morning, but no one wanted Icky to tell Mr. Kumasi that. Besides, they were beginning to see that Mr. Kumasi did things his own way. No matter what they told him, he just said, "Watch and listen." So the kids put on their jackets and followed Mr. Kumasi outside.

"In Ghana, our favorite sport is football," said Mr. Kumasi. "In this country, you call it soccer."

"We love soccer!" said Tac.

Alec tossed a soccer ball to Mr. Kumasi, who kicked it straight up into the air and caught it on his head. Somehow, he made it spin on his forehead!

"Can you teach us to do that?" asked Ettabetta.

"Yes!" said Mr. Kumasi. And everyone—except Icky—said along with him, "Watch and listen!"

Only Good Surprises

Before lunch, Mr. Kumasi read the class an African story about a spider named Anansi.

"Ms. Blossom would have had us read silently," Icky whispered to Hot Rod. "She—"

"Shh!" said Hot Rod. "I want to hear this funny story."

After lunch, Mr. Kumasi had a spelling bee.

"Ms. Blossom only has spelling bees on <u>Fridays</u>!" Icky protested to Toc.

Toc just said, "I know. It's fun to have one now."

Later, Mr. Kumasi said, "Let's do some creative writing. What shall we write?"

"Oh, Mr. Kumasi!" Icky burst out. "Ms. Blossom <u>tells</u> us what to write, like letters, or poems, or reports. She'd be surprised if we wrote just any old thing!"

"Doesn't Ms. Blossom like surprises?" Mr. Kumasi asked.

"Only <u>good</u> surprises," said Icky.

"Then let's give her one," said Mr. Kumasi. He smiled at Icky. "Let's write get-well cards to her. I will deliver them myself."

"Hooray!" cheered the class. And this time, even Icky was happy!

Get Well Soon!

Here's a bouquet to help us say
we hope you're better, day by day.
Oswald

Do you ache? Do you sneeze?
Do you cough? Do you wheeze?
Rest and then feel better, please!
Alf

Knock, Knock!
Who's there?
Atch.
Atch who?
Gesundheit!
Doc

The trick
When you're sick
Is to get better QUICK!
Lily

There once was a teacher, Ms. Blossom,
Whose students all thought she was awesome.
When she got the flu,
They said, "What we'll do
Is send her some flowers—we'll draw some!"
Toc

Roses are red,
Violets are blue,
We're sorry that
You have the flu.
Tic

Tea and honey,
A soft warm bed,
Lots of pillows for your head.
Sleep and dream,
And, when you rise,
Sunshine in the
Bright blue skies.
Tac

When your nose is stuffy,
It's hard not to be sad.
So go ahead and blow it,
Then you won't feel so bad!
Sal

I'll never have a cold I like.
I'll never have a fever.
And if a flu bug flies near me
I'll run away and leave her.
Hot Rod

Don't be sick!
Get well quick!
Alec

All the students in your class
Hope your illness soon will pass.
— Mr. Kumasi

Q: When is your throat like a pony?
A: When it's a little hoarse!
Cass

92

Ms. Blossom, Ms. Blossom,
Where are you?
When you're not in school,
We don't know what to do.
Come back, come back,
to our class and me.
We'll be the best students
you ever did see.
Ettabetta

Chicken soup with lots of rice
When you're sick tastes very nice.
Frits

mmm mmm
chicken soup!

I get
well

Achoo! Poor you!
You've got the flu!
Stay home for a day or two - but only a few
because.
WE MISS YOU!
(Though Mr. Kumasi is pretty nice, too!)
Icky

Achoo!
Achoo!
Achoo!

Chapter 25

Springing Spring

A brisk, bouncy breeze was blowing the day Ms. Blossom came back. She opened a window to let in some fresh air.

"Spring is beginning to spring," she said.

"Look!" said Tic. "I'm a springing spring." Tic bent down and sprang up, bent down and sprang up. "Boing, boing, boing!" she said.

Tac said, "I'm a falling fall." Tac leaned

sideways off her chair until she fell on the floor. CLONK!

Toc said, "I'm a marching March!" Toc marched around the room, saying, "Left, right, left, right!"

"I think you girls have spring fever," said Ms. Blossom.

"What's that?" asked Frits.

"It's a wiggly, rambunctious feeling," said Ms. Blossom. "And the only cure is exercise and sunshine. So let's all go to the roof and check our garden. March quietly."

Queen Bee

The Superkids were clearing dead leaves out of the long boxes when suddenly Tac shrieked, "Eek! A bee!"

"Help!" yelped Toc.

"It's dead," Tic said. She picked up the bee and held it gently. "But it's a beauty."

"Cool!" said Alf. "I didn't know you liked bees, Tic."

"I do," said Tic. "A lot."

"You <u>do</u>?" said Toc with surprise. "But bees sting."

"Not all bees," said Tic. "Different bees do different things."

"One bee is the queen," Alf began. "She—"

"The queen?" Tac interrupted. "Now <u>that's</u> the job for me." Tac put her scarf on her head like a crown and fluttered her arms. "Buzz, buzz! Look at me! I'm a bee-yoo-tiful queen bee."

Toc and Tac laughed, but Alf and Tic kept looking at the bee.

Alf said, "Tic, next time we go to the media center, I'll show you a site about honeybees that I found on the Internet."

"Great!" said Tic.

Tac and Toc looked at each other. They didn't get it. What was so great about bees?

The Bee Team

Tic, Tac, and Toc always walked to school together. But the next morning Tic wasn't at their usual meeting spot. When the other girls got to school, they saw Tic and Alf on the playground looking at the grass with a magnifying glass.

"Tic, you didn't tell us you were coming early," Tac said crossly. "What are you doing?"

"Looking for bees," said Tic.

"You're kidding!" said Toc. "What are you two, the Bee Team?"

Tic and Alf grinned at each other. "If we are, we're not a very good team," said Alf. "We haven't found a single bee."

"It's too cold," said Tic. "Let's try after school. It'll be warmer."

"You can't, Tic," said Toc, sounding bossy. "We planned to practice batting after school. Remember?"

"Oh, right," said Tic with a little frown. "You two start practicing without me. I'll come later."

Now Tac and Toc were mad. It was clear that Tic was more interested in bees than in batting!

Buzz Off!

Tic, Tac, and Toc were looking at a horse book when Alf said, "Tic, come look at this website about bees."

Tic jumped up. "Does it show bees dancing?" she said.

"Do bees dance?" said Toc, giggling. She and Tac waved their arms and twirled, pretending they were dancing bees.

"Quit it," said Tic, annoyed.

"Bees don't exactly <u>dance</u>," Alf explained. "They move to tell each other where to find pollen for honey."

"I read a book about a bear who ate so much honey that he got stuck in a doorway," said Tac.

"Let's find it," said Toc. "Come on, Tic."

"Not now," said Tic. "Stop telling me what to do!" She stormed off.

"Oh! Sorry!" Tac called after her in a snippy way. "We forgot that you and Alf are the important Bee Team. Toc and I will just buzz off!"

"What's the matter with you guys?" asked Alf. "Tic can be interested in bees and still be your friend too."

101

To Bee or Not to Bee

Tac and Toc were playing catch after school while Tic looked for bees with Alf. "I don't want our friendship with Tic to fall apart," said Tac.

"Me either," said Toc sadly.

Tac stooped to pick up the ball, then froze. "Yikes!" she yelped. "A bee!" Gently, she put her glove over it. "Get Tic!"

Toc shot off and was back in a flash with Tic and Alf. They bent down and peeked under the glove. The bee rose slowly, then floated away.

"Cool!" sighed Alf.

"<u>Really</u> cool," sighed Tic. She smiled at Tac and Toc. "You guys are a better bee team than we are," she said. "I thought you didn't like bees."

"We don't!" said Tac. "But you <u>do</u>, and we like <u>you</u>."

Chapter 26

Oswald's Invitation

One day after school, Oswald said to Cass, "I'm having a birthday party a week from Saturday. Do you want to come?"

"Sure!" said Cass.

"Good," said Oswald. "Maybe we'll play basketball or go to a movie or something."

"That sounds good," said Cass. "I'll ask my mom if I can come. I'll let you know tomorrow."

"OK," said Oswald. "See you later."

"Bye!" said Cass. "And thanks!"

Cass ran off to meet Ana before Brownies. "Sorry I'm late," she said to Ana. "I was talking to Oswald. He invited me to his birthday party. It's a week from Saturday."

"Oh, Cass!" said Ana. "You didn't tell Oswald you'd go, did you?"

Ana's Advice

"Sure," said Cass. "I told Oswald I'll go to his party if my mom says I can. Why wouldn't I go?"

"Well," said Ana. "At my school, girls don't go to boys' parties in the second grade."

"But," sputtered Cass, "I went to Oswald's party last year."

"Last year you were in <u>first</u> grade," Ana pointed out. "Did Oswald say he was going to invite any other girls?"

"Uh, no," said Cass.

"Eww!" said Ana. "Then you'll probably be the only girl there."

"Oh, eeeeeww!" said Cass. "How can I get out of going?"

"My mom and I are going hiking that Saturday," said Ana. "Tell Oswald you can't go to his party because you're coming with us."

107

A Little Uncomfortable

When Cass got home from Brownies, she called Tac. "Did Oswald invite you to his birthday party?" she asked.

"No," said Tac. "Maybe it's only for boys. My sister told me that's what happens in second grade."

So Ana is right! thought Cass.

The next morning, Cass spoke to Oswald while they were feeding the fish. "I'm sorry, but I can't come to your party," Cass said. "I forgot that Ana invited me to go hiking that Saturday."

"Oh," said Oswald. He sounded disappointed. "That's too bad."

Cass felt a little uncomfortable. But she was sure that she was right to follow Ana's advice. It was better to be a little uncomfortable now than to be really uncomfortable later at Oswald's party!

Go, Go, Go!

SMACK! Cass hit the ball. She dropped the bat and began to run. Halfway around the bases she slowed down, but her teammates yelled, "Go, go, go!" So Cass kept going and flew across home plate.

"Home run!" yelled the Superkids. "Yay, Cass!"

"Good going," said Doc as Cass sat on the bench.

Cass grinned. "I love baseball," she said.

"I know," said Doc. "It's really too bad you aren't going to Oswald's party."

"What do you mean?" asked Cass.

"Oswald's dad is taking us all to a Roosters game," said Doc.

"<u>What</u>?" gasped Cass. The Roosters were the local baseball team. Their games were terrific! Cass loved the Roosters! She was a Rooster Booster.

"But I thought second-grade girls didn't <u>go</u> to boys' parties," she said weakly.

"They go if the whole class is invited," said Doc. "Oswald mailed invitations to everybody. I bet they come today."

For Cass

Hey, Rooster Booster!
Please come to my birthday party!
Meet at my house Saturday at 2:00.
Dad will drive us to Roosters Field.

Bring your mitt!
You might catch a foul ball!

Oswald

Cock-a-doodle-don't

"Cock-a-doodle-doo!
Cock-a-doodle-crow!
Roosters! Roosters!
Go! Go! Go!"

It was lunchtime on the day after everyone received Oswald's invitation, and the kids were yelling the Roosters cheer. They were so excited about the party that they couldn't talk about anything else. Cass felt left out.

Alf said, "I bet the Roosters announcer will wish Oswald a happy birthday over the microphone."

"They'll flash Oswald's name in lights on the scoreboard!" said Alec.

"Maybe they'll let us run the bases between innings," said Tic, "and give us bobblehead Roosters or Rooster Booster T-shirts!"

"Everyone will sing the special Roosters happy birthday song," said Icky.

The kids sang:

"Happy birthday to you,
Cock-a-doodle-doodle-doodle-doo!
Happy birthday, dear Oswald!
From the Roosters to you!"

The more the kids cheered "Cock-a-doodle-doo," the more miserable Cass felt. *Please!* she thought. *Cock-a-doodle-don't!*

Chapter 27

Persuasion

"When you <u>persuade</u> someone, you talk them into doing something. You convince them," Ms. Blossom said. "Today you'll learn about writing persuasive paragraphs. Who'll give me an example of persuasion?"

"Well," said Frits. "When Cass hit the ball and ran to second base, we yelled, 'Go, go, go!' and <u>persuaded</u> her to keep running. She got a home run!"

"Splendid!" said Ms. Blossom.

"But persuasion isn't always good," said Cass, thinking about how Ana had persuaded her not to go to Oswald's party. "Sometimes someone's wrong, and talks you out of doing something fun."

"That's true," said Ms. Blossom. "Persuasion is something to be careful of. It's good to listen to other people's advice, but we do have to think for ourselves."

"What will we write our paragraphs about?" asked Alec.

"Food," said Ms. Blossom. "You'll try to persuade

the class that your favorite food is the best. Then we'll vote, and have the winning food as a snack."

"Great!" said Alec, and no one had to be persuaded to agree.

Ms. Blossom's Idea

Cass met with Ms. Blossom to discuss her ideas for her paragraph about popcorn. "The best popcorn is at Roosters Field," said Cass. "Everyone will have some at Oswald's party. But I can't go."

"Ah, yes," said Ms. Blossom. "You're hiking instead."

"I wish I weren't," said Cass. "I really want to go to Oswald's party. Do you think I could tell Ana and Oswald that I've changed my mind?"

"No," said Ms. Blossom. "Once you say no to an invitation, that's that."

"Well," replied Cass. "I wasn't quite telling the truth when I said that Ana had <u>already</u> invited me to go hiking."

"Not quite telling the truth is lying, and lying always leads to trouble," said Ms. Blossom.

Cass nodded miserably.

"You can't go to Oswald's party," said Ms. Blossom. "But you're still his friend. Maybe you could find a way to show him that you're happy it's his birthday."

"Thanks," said Cass as she gave Ms. Blossom a hug.

Batting Advice

Sal swung fast. WHIFF! He missed.

"Strike three!" yelled the umpire. "You're out!"

Sal frowned as he walked to the bench. He'd struck out <u>again</u>. He used to be the best batter on the team. But this spring he'd missed almost every pitch.

"Shake it off," said Hot Rod.

"Bend your knees next time," said Doc.

"Everybody has slumps," said Oswald.

"Lift your left elbow more," said Frits.

Sal knew his friends were trying to help, but he wished they'd stop giving him advice. It made him nervous.

As Sal walked home after the game, Cass called, "Wait for me!"

Sal waited for Cass to catch up. Then he waited for her to say something about his batting, like everybody else. But Cass was quiet.

"Aren't you going to give me any advice?" Sal asked.

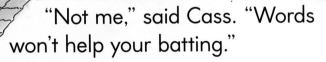

"Not me," said Cass. "Words won't help your batting."

"<u>That</u>," said Sal, "is the first helpful thing I've heard all day!"

Bumpy

The Superkids were supposed to work on their persuasive paragraphs all afternoon, but Sal wrote his quickly. He was too discouraged about his batting to be enthusiastic about anything—even chocolate-chip cookies.

When all the kids had finished their drafts, they met with partners who asked questions about their paragraphs so they could make changes. Sal's partner was Ettabetta. First, Sal skimmed Ettabetta's paragraph about grapes. "It's fine," he said. "You get a star for being specific. I don't have any questions. How's my paragraph?"

"You get a star for being clear about your topic," said Ettabetta. "And I have two questions about your paragraph. Can you describe the cookies better? And can you tell why you like them?"

"I said they're good," said Sal.

"Ms. Blossom told us not to use words like 'good,'"

said Ettabetta. "We're supposed to tell how our foods look, smell, taste, and feel."

"Feel?" asked Sal. "How does a chocolate-chip cookie <u>feel</u>?"

"Bumpy?" suggested Ettabetta.

"OK," sighed Sal. "I'll add that."

"And I circled your spelling mistakes," said Ettabetta, "so you can fix them too."

"OK," Sal sighed again. *First my batting. Now my writing,* he thought. *I can't do <u>anything</u> right!*

Enjoy the Cookie

The next day, Sal was leaving the lunch table when Ettabetta said, "Wait."

"Now what?" groaned Sal.

"Dessert!" said Ettabetta. She handed Sal a homemade chocolate-chip cookie.

"Thanks!" said Sal. He sat back down.

Sal started to eat, but Ettabetta said, "Not so fast!" She took out paper and a pencil. "First tell me how the cookie looks."

"It's golden brown," said Sal.

Ettabetta wrote *golden brown*. "Now take a bite," she said. "Don't rush. Think, then tell me how the cookie tastes and feels."

Sal chewed slowly, then said, "I never noticed this before, but the cookie part is soft and sweet, and the chip part is hard and a little bitter."

"Great!" said Ettabetta, writing down Sal's words. "How does it smell?"

"Chocolatey," he sighed happily.

"Excellent!" said Ettabetta. "You knew what to write all along. You just needed to slow down and enjoy the cookie!"

Chapter 28

Vote!

Let's Have Naan by Toc

Naan is bread from India. Naan feels soft, fluffy, and warm. It smells like fresh-baked bread and looks like a pancake.
Vote for Naan!

naan bread

Toc

popcorn by Cass

Want something corny, salty, buttery, and soft? Then vote for popcorn! Every kernel is light, white, and fluffy as a cloud. Have a handful! Close your eyes, and you'll think you're at a Roosters Game!
popcorn is fun!

mmmm!

yum! yum!

I Think We Should Have Pretzels
by Frits

Pretzels are mouth-watering. They are thin and salty, and when you bite them, they go CRUNCH! I love pretzels, and you will, too.

crunch! crunch!

Pretzels crunch

You're Going to Like Awesome Grapes
by Ettabetta

What are smooth on the outside, juicy on the inside, and squishy when you squeeze them? Grapes! They are green or bluish purple. Grapes are small, so you'll get a lot of them. Vote for grapes. They're healthy!

125

More Food!

Vote for Carrots and Ranch Dip
by Doc

If you like crunchy, and you like creamy, you'll like carrots and ranch dip. The carrots are **crisp** and **orange**, and the ranch dip is **smooth** and **white**. Together, they're **cool** and **tangy** on your tongue.

Try Cannoli
by Icky

You'll love cannoli! Oh, what a texture! There's a thin, sweet, crunchy crust on the outside and cold, thick cream on the inside. Take a bite and surprise your mouth.

Reach for a Peach
by Hot Rod

Fuzzy, juicy, tart, and sweet—that's what peaches are. Take a big bite, and let the juice squirt onto your chin! Vote for peaches!

Everyone Loves Chocolate-Chip Cookies   by Sal

Chocolate-chip cookies are bumpy and golden brown. The cookie part is soft and sweet, and the chip part is hard and just a little bitter. And don't you love that chocolatey smell? Mmm! Vote for chocolate-chip cookies!!

bitter   bumpy   sweet   Yum

soft   Sweet   soft

Yum   golden brown

mmm! mmm! mmm!   hard

One Smart Cookie

The Superkids published their persuasive paragraphs by putting them on the bulletin board.

"Yours is good, Sal," said Icky. "Did it take you a long time to write it?"

Sal laughed. "Yes!" he said. "I rewrote it after talking to Ettabetta. But it was fun."

"Fun?" asked Icky.

"Ettabetta made me slow down and enjoy eating a chocolate-chip cookie," explained Sal. "And that helped me slow down and enjoy <u>writing</u> about the cookie too."

"Your slow paragraph makes me want a chocolate-chip cookie—<u>fast</u>," joked Icky.

That afternoon, when it was his turn to bat, Sal remembered Ettabetta's advice about going slow. Instead of swinging at the first few pitches, he relaxed and waited. When a really good pitch came over the plate, he swung hard.

THH-WACK! Sal hit the ball and sent it flying!

Then Sal did <u>not</u> follow Ettabetta's advice about going slow. He ran as fast as he possibly could—all the way to second base!

What If?

"All right, class," said Ms. Blossom. "It's time to vote."

Ms. Blossom walked between the desks with a shoebox that had a hole in its lid. The kids put their votes in the shoebox.

"When will you tell us which food got the most votes?" Lily asked Ms. Blossom.

"I won't tell everyone," said Ms. Blossom. "I'll tell only the person who wrote about the winning food. That person will bring the food on Friday. It will be a surprise for the rest of you. We'll have the winning food as a snack in a picnic on the roof."

"What if there's a tie?" asked Frits.

"Or what if three foods all get the same number of votes?" asked Tac.

"What if some yucky food wins?" asked Alf. "That would be a terrible surprise!"

Ms. Blossom laughed. "What if, what if, what if," she said. "Wait and see. That's what surprises are all about!"

And the Winner Is . . .

On Friday, huge storm clouds hung low over the school. After lunch, it was so gloomy that Ms. Blossom had to turn on the lights. Then—CRASH! Thunder boomed. And CRACK! Lightning sliced the sky. Fat raindrops pelted against the window and soaked the ground.

"Now we can't have our picnic," wailed Doc.

"Yes, we can," said Ms. Blossom. "We'll have it inside." The children helped Ms. Blossom push the desks and chairs to the sides of the room. Cass sneaked out of the room as everyone sat, full of wiggles and giggles of excitement.

Ms. Blossom said, "The winning food is . . ." She opened the door and in came Cass with popcorn in rooster cups for everybody!

"Hooray!" the class cheered.

"Popcorn won," said Ms. Blossom. "So Cass made rooster cups for everyone."

"We'll take them to the Roosters game tomorrow," Oswald said to Cass. "Thank you!"

"You're welcome," said Cass. She and Oswald held up their cups and cheered—

Cock-a-doodle-doo!

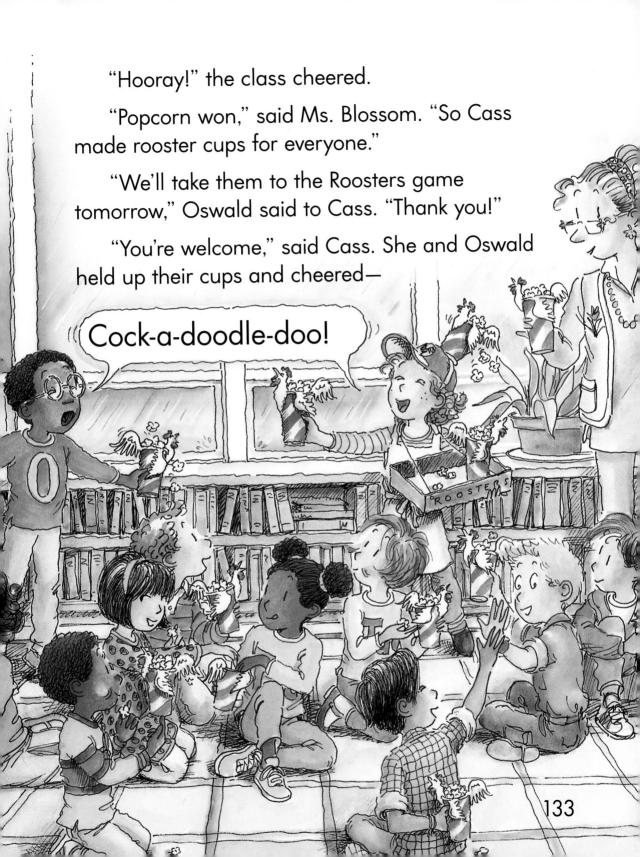

133

Chapter 29

Roboticons

"Oswald," said Ms. Blossom, "give me your Roboticon."

"OK," said Oswald. Students could play with toys from home on the playground, but if Ms. Blossom spotted a toy in the classroom, she took it away until recess. That was the rule. Oswald pretended to swim Shark onto Ms. Blossom's hand. Shark was his favorite Roboticon because he could change it from a robot into a great white shark.

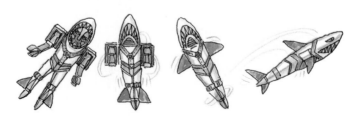

Hot Rod smiled at Oswald. He loved Roboticons too. His favorite was Speedster, because he could change it from a robot into a race car.

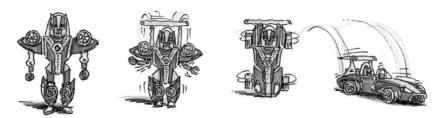

Soon it was recess. Hot Rod and Oswald met on the playground. "Let's destroy Thunderbolt," said Oswald. He held up a rock to be Thunderbolt.

Shark jumped onto Speedster. They crashed into Thunderbolt and knocked him down again and again.

"That was fun," said Hot Rod as the boys walked inside. "Let's play again tomorrow."

"OK!" said Oswald.

Shark to the Rescue

The next day before lunch, Hot Rod asked Oswald, "Did you bring Shark?"

"Yes," said Oswald. "But I'm staying inside with the Lunch Bunch to finish my math, so we can't play at recess."

"Too bad," said Hot Rod. He paused, and then asked, "May I play with Shark?"

"OK." said Oswald. He handed Shark to Hot Rod.

"Thanks!" said Hot Rod.

It had rained during the night, so there were lots of wonderful mud puddles on the playground. Hot Rod pretended that Speedster got stuck in a mud pit and began to be sucked down.

"Shark to the rescue!" shouted Hot Rod. He made Shark dive into the muck and carry Speedster safely to shore. The real mud made the pretend game so much fun that Hot Rod made Shark dive into the mud and save Speedster over and over again until recess ended.

Mud

When Hot Rod got back to the room, he tossed Shark to Oswald. "Thanks!" he said.

Oswald frowned. "What did you do to Shark?" he asked. "He's all muddy."

Hot Rod took Shark back and swiped it on his pants. "Here you go, good as new," he said, returning Shark to Oswald.

But Shark still looked terrible to Oswald. He scrubbed the toy with a tissue.

"Man! You're too fussy," said Hot Rod. "I think the mud makes Speedster look tough. Besides, a little mud never hurt anything."

"A <u>little</u> mud?" said Oswald. "There's so much mud on Shark that I can't change him from a shark to a robot anymore. You wrecked him."

"I did <u>not</u>," said Hot Rod.

"You did too," said Oswald.

"<u>Boys</u>," Ms. Blossom interrupted. "What's going on?"

Find a Way

Oswald pointed at Hot Rod. "He borrowed my Roboticon and wrecked it," he said angrily.

"I did <u>not</u> wreck it," said Hot Rod. "I just got a little mud on it."

Ms. Blossom held up her hand. "Stop," she said. "Hot Rod, when you borrow something, you must return it in good shape. You'll stay after school today and wash Oswald's Roboticon."

Oswald looked pleased.

"And Oswald, you'll stay after school too," said Ms. Blossom.

"<u>Me</u>?" asked Oswald. "What did I do?"

"It takes two to argue," said Ms. Blossom. "You boys had fun playing with your Roboticons before. Perhaps after school you can figure out how to play well again."

"But—" Oswald began.

"Find a way, or never bring another toy to school," said Ms. Blossom firmly.

Oswald and Hot Rod scowled at each other, but they knew they'd have to do what Ms. Blossom said. When Ms. Blossom spoke like that she meant it.

Bubble World

After school, Hot Rod filled the sink with soapy water and swam Shark around to give him a bath.

"Hey," said Oswald, coming to stand next to him. "Can I wash Speedster?"

Hot Rod shrugged. "If you want," he said.

The two boys stood silently as they dunked and scrubbed the Roboticons in the soapsuds.

"Look," said Oswald. "Speedster's trapped in a bubble. Make Shark pop it."

Hot Rod used Shark to free Speedster from the bubble.

Then Hot Rod said, "Wait. I've got an idea." He ran back to his cubby and returned with a straw from a juice box. He put one end in the water and blew. Bubbles burbled up and filled the sink.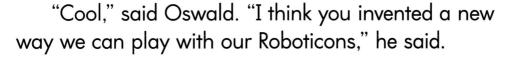

"Cool," said Oswald. "I think you invented a new way we can play with our Roboticons," he said.

"We can call it Bubble World," said Hot Rod.

"OK," agreed Oswald. "Let's start popping!"

Chapter 30

Testing Begins

Icky walked s-l-o-w-l-y to his chair in the classroom.

"Good morning, Icky," said Ms. Blossom.

Icky sighed. "Hi," he said. He sounded glum.

"What's the matter?" asked Ms. Blossom.

Icky sighed again. "We have testing today," he said. "I hate testing." Icky's hands felt sweaty and shaky. His stomach felt yucky. His brain felt empty. And his mouth felt dry.

Ms. Blossom smiled. "Maybe it would help if you thought of the test like a soccer game," she said.

"<u>What</u>?" said Icky. "I don't get it."

"Well," said Ms. Blossom, "during soccer season, you have practice every day. So when you're in a game, you know what to do. Right?"

"Right," said Icky.

"It's the same with schoolwork," said Ms. Blossom. "You learn every day. So on a test you know what to do. Right?"

"I guess so," said Icky. He grinned. Ms. Blossom's idea made him feel much better.

Magic

"Time's up, class," said Ms. Blossom. "Please put your pencils down. Pass your test booklets forward. Testing is finished."

"Hooray," cheered the Superkids, but without much oomph. They'd been testing for three days, and they were worn out.

"I'm proud of you, boys and girls," said Ms. Blossom. "And I have a treat to share with you. Line up and follow me."

Ms. Blossom led the Superkids up to the rooftop garden. "Look," she said.

"Hooray!" cheered the Superkids, and this time they sounded happy and excited. At last, at last, after all the planting
   and watering
      and weeding
         and waiting,
            their daffodils had

The Superkids stuck their noses into the big yellow daffodils and smelled their springy scent.

They goofed around, squatting down so that it looked as if the daffodils were growing out of their heads like horns or antennae.

"I can't believe those dull brown bulbs that Ms. Blossom gave us last fall turned into such pretty flowers," said Tic. "It seems like magic."

The Big Contest

GO GREEN!

Have you done something to beautify our town?

Have you done something to protect our environment?

Write an entry that describes your project. Include illustrations. Submit your entry to: **The America Goes Green Contest**

Judges will visit to select the winning projects. Winners will have a float in the town parade.

"Doc," whispered Lily. "Look at this."

Doc read the computer screen. "Are you thinking what I'm thinking?" she asked.

"Yes!" said Lily. "Let's send in an entry about our rooftop garden. And let's not tell Ms. Blossom. If we win, it will be a great surprise for her."

"OK," said Doc. "When's the deadline for the contest?"

"Well," said Lily. "That part is a surprise too, but not such a good one. The deadline is today at five."

"Yikes!" said Doc. "In that case, we need help, and we need it fast. Let's talk to everyone and make a plan."

Click on SEND

The Superkids met at the public library after school. Everyone pitched in to help write and illustrate their contest entry.

Just before five o'clock, Doc said, "Are we ready?"

"Yes!" said the kids. They squashed together and put their hands on the mouse.

"One, two, three!" said Doc.

CLICK! The kids clicked on SEND.

151

A Blooming Rooftop Garden
by the Superkids

At the beginning of second grade,
our teacher gave us daffodil bulbs.

We planted the bulbs in boxes on the roof of our school building.

We watered the bulbs. We weeded the boxes.

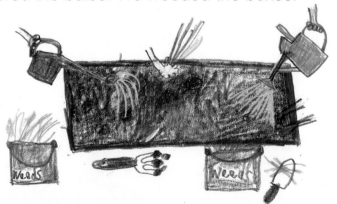

We waited all winter.

When spring came, green sprouts popped up.
Next, the daffodils grew taller. Then they had buds.
At last, the daffodils blossomed!

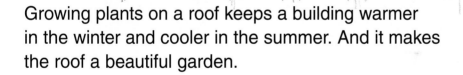

Growing plants on a roof keeps a building warmer
in the winter and cooler in the summer. And it makes
the roof a beautiful garden.

Our rooftop garden is a perfect project for our class
because guess what our teacher's name is?

Ms. Blossom!

Babies

Daffodils had blossomed on Ms. Gibson's farm too. Golly loved smells, so he enjoyed sniffing the spring air. It was a mixture of flowers, new grass, and mud. Golly also enjoyed meeting all the baby animals that were born in the spring.

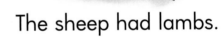

The cows had calves.   The sheep had lambs.

The hens had chicks.

The pigs had piglets.

154

But when Golly stopped by to meet Baby's goslings, the mean goose hissed. She flapped her big wings, stretched her long neck, and stabbed Golly hard with her sharp beak.

Baby chased Golly out of the barn, across the yard, past the pond, and down the road.

Golly ran. He ran so fast and so far that when he finally stopped, he didn't know where he was. Baby had disappeared. Golly sniffed to the right, and he sniffed to the left, but nothing smelled familiar.

Golly was lost.

Chapter 31

Golly on the Road

Golly sat by the road. Which way was the farm? Was it down the road or up the hill?

Golly looked for the familiar shape of the barn. But all he saw were trees bending over the road.

He listened for cows mooing and the rumble and clank of the farm tractor. But all he heard was the wind rustling in the trees.

Golly took a deep breath, hoping to smell the farm's fresh grass. But all he smelled was the dusty road and the woods behind him. Suddenly, Golly tilted his head and lifted one ear.

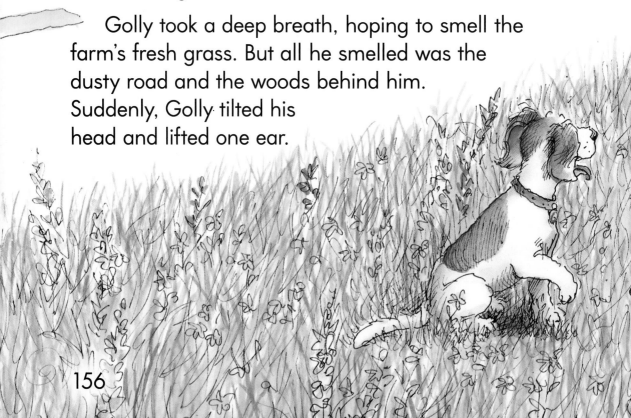

He heard a wonderful sound. It was soft at first, but it became louder and louder until *rattle-rattle-varoom!* A big yellow school bus full of noisy children chugged past.

A bus? Noisy children? Golly thought of the Superkids. He missed them with all his heart. He wasn't sure which way to go, but he knew where he wanted to be: with the Superkids. And so he began to walk, and walk, and walk, and walk, and walk, and . . .

Field Day

Back at school, the Superkids were getting ready for Field Day. They loved Field Day, but this year they were a bit sad as they stood in line waiting to go outside. A couple of days had passed, and they had heard nothing from the judges of the America Goes Green Contest. "I guess they're not interested," sighed Lily.

"It would have been fun to surprise Ms. Blossom," said Icky.

"And to be in the parade," added Doc.

Everyone was disappointed. They'd worked so hard on their entry!

But it was hard to stay disappointed once the games began. The day was hot and sunny. The playground was divided into different stations. At each station, there was something fun to do. Just about everything was wonderfully wet and messy!

159

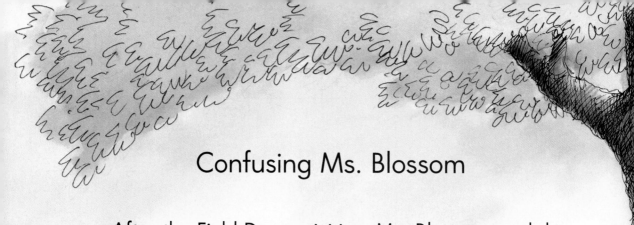

Confusing Ms. Blossom

After the Field Day activities, Ms. Blossom and the Superkids flopped down in the shade. They were eating lime Popsicles when Mr. Martinez, the principal, came over. He had two women with him.

"Ms. Blossom," said Mr. Martinez, "these two ladies have just looked at your rooftop garden."

"Oh?" said Ms. Blossom. She was confused.

"We're judges from the America Goes Green Contest," said the tall woman. "We thought your entry was excellent." She handed the entry to Ms. Blossom.

"<u>My</u> entry?" said Ms. Blossom, even more confused. The Superkids hid their smiles behind their Popsicles. "I don't know anything about this," she said. "Who sent this entry in to your contest?"

"We did!" the Superkids exploded.

"Well!" said Ms. Blossom. "This is splendid, just splendid!"

"We think your garden is splendid too," said the tall woman. "We have come to a decision on the America Goes Green Contest. I am pleased to tell you that you win!"

Showers

"WE WON!" shouted the Superkids. "We'll have a float in the parade!" They jumped up and down and hugged one another. They hugged Ms. Blossom. They hugged Mr. Martinez. They even hugged the judges.

Then everyone went up to the rooftop garden, and one of the judges said, "Please line up to have your picture taken for the contest website."

"Uh-oh," said Sal. "We're a mess!"

He was right. All the kids had muddy hands and feet, grimy faces, and lime-green mouths.

"Quick!" said Ms. Blossom. She turned on the hose. "Stand under the spray."

The water was cold. "Eek!" the Superkids shrieked. They hurried to scrub their hands and faces, and to slick back their hair. Ms. Blossom sprayed herself too. Then everyone stood behind the banner to hide their muddy shirts and grass-stained shorts. They hid their shoes behind the daffodils.

This is what the photograph looked like on the contest website:

THE AMERICA GOES GREEN CONTEST WINNERS!

Ms. Blossom and her second graders won the America Goes Green Contest. As their prize, these super kids will have a float in the parade next Saturday.

"Oh, No!"

The next morning, the Superkids were planning their float for the parade when Ms. Blossom was called out of the room. When she returned, she looked pale. "Boys and girls," she said. "I have some bad news. Ms. Gibson called. Golly is missing."

"Oh, no!" gasped the Superkids. "Golly's lost?"

Ms. Blossom nodded. "He has been missing for a couple of days," she said. "At first, Ms. Gibson thought he'd turn up at the farm, but now she thinks he might be on his way back here."

"Maybe he's running away from Baby, that horrible goose," said Tac.

"I bet Baby chased him away," said Oswald.

"Golly is a smart dog," said Ms. Blossom. "He'll figure out what to do."

"We've <u>got</u> to find Golly," said Alf.

"Or help him find <u>us</u>," said Sal.

164

165

Chapter 32

Looking for Golly

The Superkids and Ms. Blossom did everything they could think of to find Golly. They searched the roads near the farm with Gus and Gert.

They made posters and signs and put them up all over.

They sent out e-mail notices.

They telephoned neighbors.

They visited animal shelters in case someone had found Golly and brought him in.

They rode their bikes through town calling for Golly.

They took turns sitting by the club bus in case Golly came there.

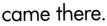 

Tired, Lonely, and Sad

And where was Golly? He was walking down a sidewalk next to a busy road. He had found his way to town, but he was just as lost as ever. Cars swished past, blowing grit and dust in his eyes. His paws were sore, and his legs were tired. But Golly walked on until

at last the sun began to set. Then he collapsed in a heap next to a dumpster.

As the sky became darker and the streetlights

went on, Golly felt more and more lonely and sad. He missed the safe, warm barn. He missed the comforting sounds of the animals. He missed the horses' gentle breathing. He missed the owls' soft hooting and the sheep sighing in their sleep.

Here in town, it was never quiet. Cars honked and sirens blared. Often, Golly heard music, and people laughing and talking and calling out to one another. But he never heard anyone calling out to him.

Golly curled up and rested his nose on his paws. He was tired, hungry, thirsty, and lost. But Golly was a brave dog. As soon as the sun rose, he would start walking again, looking for the Superkids. And he wouldn't stop until he found them.

The Superkids' Float

The Superkids and Ms. Blossom were quiet while they decorated their float that Friday. The flowery float looked great, but no one could feel excited. They were all too sad about Golly.

They were even sadder when they gathered at the float Saturday morning before the parade.

"Look," cried Ettabetta. "Our float is ruined!"

"And we thought things couldn't get worse," moaned Sal.

It had been very windy during the night, and their float was wrecked. The green streamers drooped in ripped shreds, and most of the yellow crepe-paper blossoms had blown away.

"What'll we do?" asked Icky as the kids pulled the ruined streamers off the float. "Should we forget about being in the parade?"

"No," said Alf. "The contest is counting on us."

"But we don't have time to decorate our float again," said Toc.

"Let's not cry over spilled milk," said Ms. Blossom. "We'll just have to make the best of it. Climb on up. Our float isn't a flop as long as we're on it."

The Parade Begins!

Boom! thumped the drums in the marching band.

Toot, tootle, toot! honked the horns.

Snap! flapped the flags in the cool, brisk breeze.

"Hooray!" cheered the crowd that lined the streets.

When the Superkids' float got to the judges' stand, it stopped, and the kids began to sing:

"And so-o-o-o
We're the Superkids!
Every single one of us
Is fabulous and marvelous—"

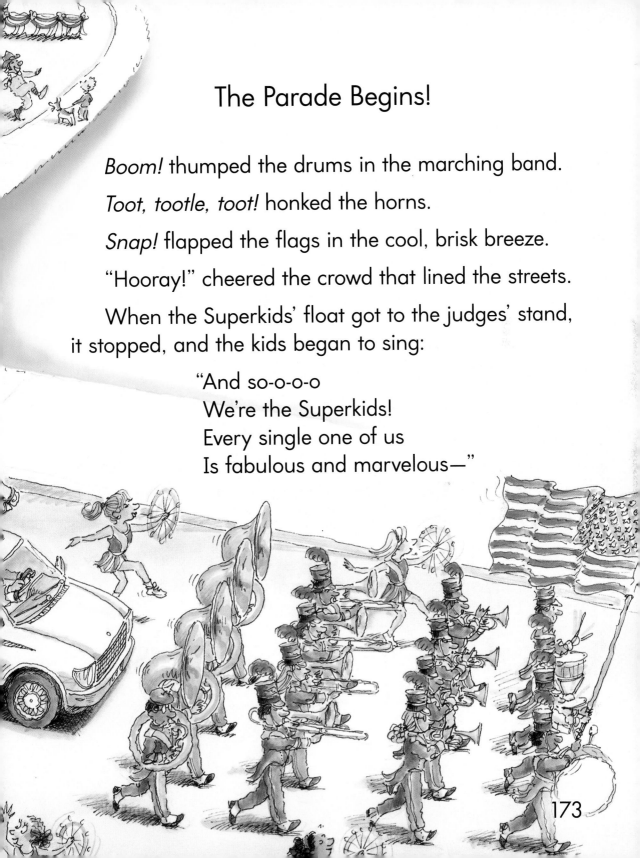

Suddenly—"Woof, woof!"—came a wonderful, familiar bark.

"What's that?" said Alf.

"Woof! Woof!" The bark came again. And, then, bounding through the crowd came

Golly!

The Superkids jumped off the float and ran to him.

"Golly, Golly, Golly!" they exclaimed. They hugged him and petted him and hugged him some more. Golly wiggled and wriggled with joy. He licked the kids' faces and smiled his wide, doggy smile.

"Oh, Golly! We are so glad to see you!" said Ms. Blossom. "Come on! You can be on the float too."

So Golly jumped up on the float, and the Superkids took their places and sang their song louder than ever:

"And so-o-o-o
We're the Superkids!
Every single one of us
Is fabulous and marvelous
And generous and courteous
And mischievous and curious!
And though there are a lot of us,
There's not a hippopotamus!
Come on, this is ridiculous!
It's really quite conspicuous;
We're just a troop of
Soooo-per doooo-per kids!"

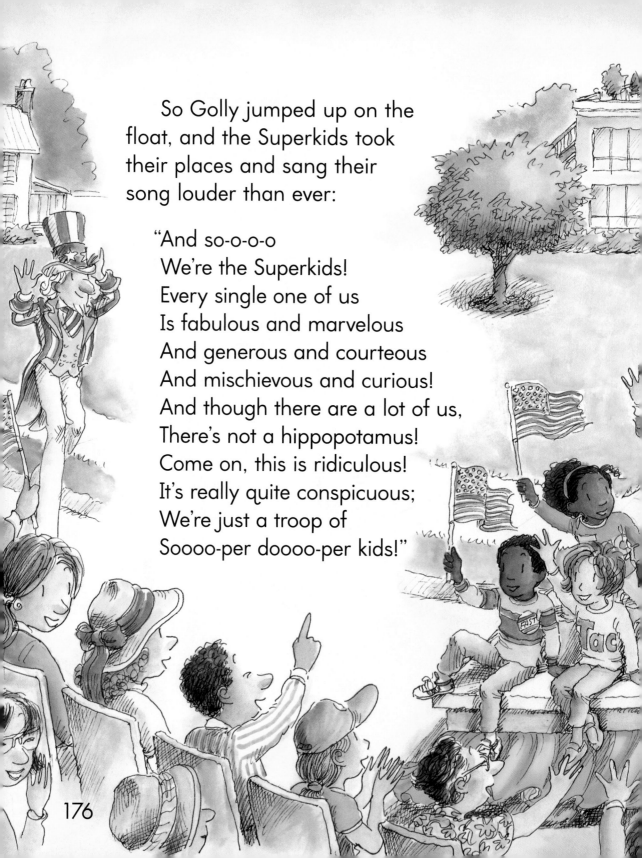

177

Goodbye

After the parade, Ms. Blossom and the Superkids gathered on the playground at school with Golly.

"Where will Golly go now?" asked Toc.

"He doesn't have to go back to the farm, does he?" asked Oswald.

Alf added, "We don't want to have to say goodbye to him again."

"I'm afraid you'll have to," said Ms. Blossom. "In fact, you'll have to say goodbye to Golly <u>and</u> me. You'll be third graders next year."

The Superkids sighed sadly.

Ms. Blossom smiled. She knelt down and put her arm around Golly. "But you'll only have to say goodbye to Golly and me for the summer," she said. "I've decided that Golly is going to be my dog.

He'll live at my house. When school starts up again in the fall, Golly can come to school with me sometimes and spend the day on the roof in the sunshine. You can visit him there. What do you think of that?"

The Superkids burst into cheers. "Hooray!" they cheered. "That's splendid, just splendid!"